SOUND *Artistry*
INTERMEDIATE METHOD
for OBOE

PETER BOONSHAFT & CHRIS BERNOTAS

in collaboration with
DR. JUNG CHOI

Thank you for making *Sound Artistry Intermediate Method for Oboe* a part of your continued development as a musician. This book will help you progress toward becoming a more able and independent musician, focusing on both your technical and musical abilities. It offers material ranging from intermediate to advanced, making it valuable for musicians at various experience levels.

The many instrument-specific exercises in this book will help to support your personal improvement of techniques on your instrument, focusing on skills that may not always be addressed in an ensemble or in other repertoire. You will notice there are many performance and technique suggestions throughout the book. This wonderful advice has been provided by our renowned collaborative partners, as well as the many specialist teachers we worked with to create this book.

Sound Artistry Intermediate Method for Oboe is organized into lessons that can be followed sequentially. As you progress through each lesson, it is a good idea to go back to previous lessons to reinforce concepts and skills, or just to enjoy performing the music. Exercises include Long Tones, Flexibility, Major and Minor Scales (all forms), Scale Studies, Arpeggio Studies, Chromatic Studies, Etudes, and Duets, as well as exercises that are focused on skills that are particular to your instrument. You will notice that many studies are clearly marked with dynamics, articulations, style, and tempo for you to practice those aspects of performance. Other studies are intentionally left for you to determine those aspects of your musical interpretation and performance. This book progresses through various meters and every key. Once a key has been introduced, previous keys are interspersed throughout for reinforcement and variety. In the back of this book you will also find expanded-range scale pages and a detailed fingering chart.

We wish you all the best as you continue to develop your musicianship, technique, and artistry!

~ Peter Boonshaft and Chris Bernotas

Jung Choi is Assistant Professor of Oboe at the University of North Texas and enjoys a versatile career as a performer and educator. She was the associate principal oboist for the Korean National Symphony Orchestra and served as an assistant professor of oboe at Missouri State University. She regularly appears nationally and internationally as a recitalist, judge, and clinician. Currently, she also serves as the principal oboist for the Richardson Symphony.

alfred.com

Copyright © 2023 by Alfred Music
All rights reserved. Printed in USA.

No part of this book shall be reproduced, arranged, adapted, recorded, publicly performed, stored in a retrieval system, or transmitted by any means without written permission from the publisher. In order to comply with copyright laws, please apply for such written permission and/or license by contacting the publisher at alfred.com/permissions.

ISBN-10: 1-4706-6651-0
ISBN-13: 978-1-4706-6651-4

Instrument photos provided courtesy of Jupiter Band Instruments/KHS America

Lesson 1

1   **LONG TONES**—*Practice this exercise with a metronome.*

2   **LONG TONES: CHROMATIC**

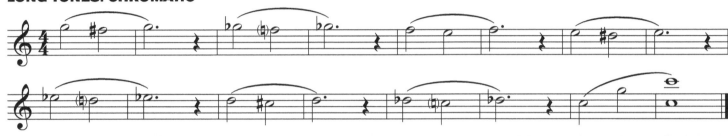

> Try this reed exercise: Take your reed only. Can you play a "C" on the reed? Now play a "G" on the reed. You might have to push the reed further out of your mouth. Connect the two pitches and slide up and down on the reed. Be aware of the reed placement on your lip. Does the reed stay on the same spot?

3   **FLEXIBILITY**—*While practicing the flexibility exercises in this book, pay close attention to the placement of the reed on the lip. One purpose of flexibility exercises is to help you find the right placement of the reed in different registers.*

4   **C MAJOR SCALE AND ARPEGGIO**—*For all scale exercises that are written in octaves, practice each octave separately and then as a two-octave scale and arpeggio.*

5   **C MAJOR SCALE STUDY**

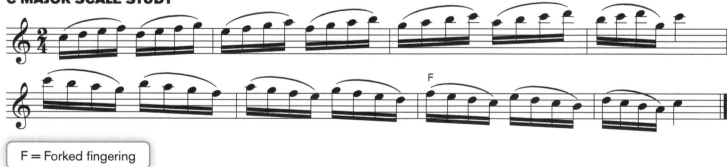

F = Forked fingering

6   **ARPEGGIO STUDY**

7 **ETUDE**—*Play all etudes slowly with a steady tempo and good tone quality before speeding up. Always keep a good tone in mind and perform with musicality.*

8 **ETUDE**

9 **ETUDE**—*Practice this etude with two-bar phrases and then four-bar phrases.*

10 **DUET**

Lesson 2

11 **A MINOR SCALE**—*Practice all of the scales in this book both all slurred and all tongued.*

12 **FORKED**—*Use the forked F fingering for all Fs in this exercise.*

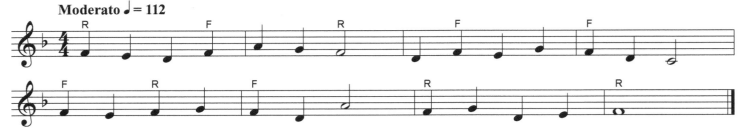

13 **FORKED**—*Use the indicated fingering for all Fs in this exercise. R is right and F is forked. Forked F exercises can be substituted as left F exercises, if you have the left F key on your oboe.*

14 **A MINOR SCALE STUDY**

15 **ETUDE**

16 CHROMATIC SCALE

17 CHROMATIC SCALE ETUDE

Moderately ♩ = 88

18 ETUDE

Lightly ♪ = 120

19 ETUDE—*After playing this etude as written, create or improvise a new ending for the last two measures.*

Moderately ♩ = 100

Lesson 3

20 **LONG TONES**—*Remember to always have proper posture, embouchure, and hand position to promote performing with a beautiful tone.*

21 **FLEXIBILITY**

22 **F MAJOR SCALE AND ARPEGGIO**—*Sing or hum these notes before playing them. Internalizing the pitch will help develop your aural skills.*

23 **F MAJOR SCALE STUDY**

24 **ETUDE**

25 **ARPEGGIO STUDY**

26 **ETUDE**

27 **DUET**

Lesson 4

28 **D MINOR SCALE**

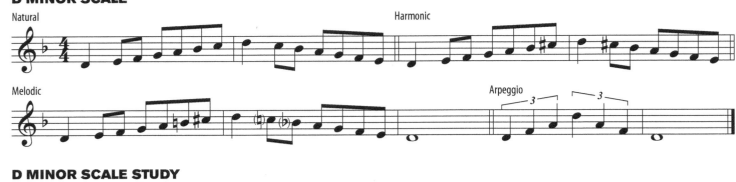

29 **D MINOR SCALE STUDY**

Moderately ♩ = 80

30 **ETUDE**

Legato ♩ = 78

31 **ETUDE**

Moderately ♩ = 88

32 **DUET**—*Work towards matching each of the musical elements in this duet for a unified performance.*

33 **ETUDE**—*Play this etude with an eighth-note pulse until the rhythm is accurate. Then, transition to the dotted-quarter-note pulse.*

Lesson 5

37 ETUDE

Stately ♩ = 98

38 DUET

Maestoso ♩ = 72

39 ETUDE

Cantabile ♩ = 72

Lesson 6

40 **FLEXIBILITY**—*Strive to maintain tone quality and keep the sound as even as possible.*

41 **G MAJOR SCALE AND ARPEGGIO**

42 **G MAJOR SCALE STUDY**—*Using manuscript paper or notation software, compose a new scale study that you think is even more challenging.*

43 **RANGE EXTENSION**

44 **RANGE EXTENSION**—*Vibrato often enhances tone quality and expression. To begin developing vibrato, try the following: Set a metronome to ♩ = 60 and play four vibrato pulses on each quarter note. Make sure to count them. The purpose of this exercise is to train your vibrato muscles. Continue to speed up the vibrato to make as musical a sound as possible. Then, try playing this exercise with vibrato.*

45 INTERVAL STUDY

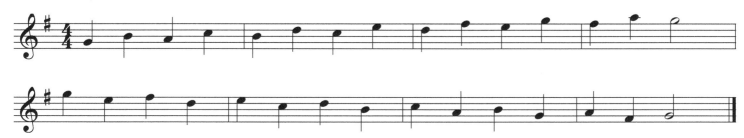

46 ETUDE

Andantino ♩ = 80

47 ETUDE—*Practice this etude with two-bar phrases and then four-bar phrases.*

Dolce ♩ = 92–100

48 ETUDE

Moderately ♩ = 112

14

Lesson 7

49 **FLEXIBILITY**

50 **E MINOR SCALE**

51 **E MINOR SCALE STUDY**

52 **ETUDE**

53 **FORKED F**—*Use the indicated fingering for the Fs in this exercise.*

54 **ETUDE**

55 **ETUDE**—*After successfully playing this etude, seek guidance from a teacher for ways you can refine your performance.*

56 **ETUDE**

Lesson 8

57 **FLEXIBILITY**

58 **B♭ MAJOR SCALE AND ARPEGGIO**

59 **B♭ MAJOR SCALE STUDY**

60 **ETUDE**—*If this exercise is not rhythmically even at the dotted-quarter-note pulse, try setting your metronome to the eighth-note pulse of ♪ = 180.*

61 **ETUDE**—*Figure out where to use forked Fs in this etude, then mark them accordingly. Be creative with the musicality of this etude by altering and adding your own dynamic markings.*

Lesson 9

GRACE NOTES are ornaments that are performed before the beat or on the beat depending on the musical time period, style, context, and notation. The last example below shows how unslashed grace notes would be performed in the Classical period. Listen to music from various historical periods and notice the different approaches to the performance of grace notes.

Most often performed before the beat

Classical period, no slash. On the beat (in time).

66 **GRACE NOTES**—*Play these grace notes just before the main note.*

67 **ETUDE**

68 **ETUDE**—*An appoggiatura is a grace note without a slash that is played on the beat. In this exercise, measures 1 and 5, as well as measures 3 and 7, would be played the same.*

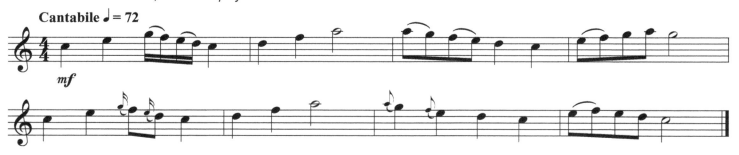

69 **ETUDE**

70 **ETUDE**

71 **ETUDE**

72 **ETUDE**—*Record your performance of this etude. Recognize the personal musical growth you have made from when you sight-read the piece. Think about the technical and musical ways your performance has improved. Do you hear a difference?*

73 **ETUDE**

Lesson 10

74 **LONG TONES**

78 CHROMATIC SCALE

79 CHROMATIC RANGE—*Remember to pay attention to the placement of the reed.*

80 MAJOR SCALE RANGE

81 DUET

Andante ♩ = 108

Lesson 11

82 **FLEXIBILITY**

83 **D MAJOR SCALE AND ARPEGGIO**

84 **D MAJOR SCALE STUDY**

Moderately ♩ = 120

85 **ETUDE**

Adagio ♩ = 60

86 **ETUDE**

Allegro ♩ = 90

continued on next page

87 ETUDE

Andante ♩ = 100

88 ETUDE—*After performing this etude, discuss the various elements of the musical work with a peer or teacher.*

Moderato ♩ = 88

89 ETUDE

Briskly ♩. = 80

Lesson 12

90 **FLEXIBILITY**—*Be mindful of your half-hole (left index finger) movement.*

91 **B MINOR SCALE**

92 **B MINOR SCALE STUDY**

93 **B MINOR SCALE STUDY**

94 **DUET**

A **TRILL** is an ornament that is performed by alternating rapidly between the written note and the next diatonic note above. Sometimes you will see a natural, sharp, or flat sign with a trill, which means to alternate between the written note and the next altered note. Always check the key signature. Find various options of trill fingerings online.

95 **TRILLS**—*Use your metronome to ensure an even and consistent rhythm.*

96 **TRILLS**—*Practice this exercise to ensure your trills are played evenly. Once you are comfortable with this exercise as written, try playing it in cut time (♩=160).*

97 **TRILLS**—*Practice measures 1–5 at a slow tempo to reinforce muscle memory, gradually increasing the tempo. This exercise will help ensure that your trills are played evenly. The trills in this exercise all use the regular fingerings, except for the C to D. Be sure to look online for the trill fingering.*

98 **ETUDE**—*Depending on the style or historical context, a trill may start with an upper neighbor as shown here. Practice these trills with and without the upper neighbor. Also, grace notes are often used at the end of a trill. This ornament is also known as a nachschläge.*

Lesson 13

99 FLEXIBILITY

100 Eb MAJOR SCALE AND ARPEGGIO

101 Eb MAJOR SCALE STUDY

102 ETUDE—*Figure out where to use forked Fs in this etude, then mark them accordingly.*

103 ETUDE

104 **DUET**

Lesson 14

105 **LONG TONES**

106 **FLEXIBILITY**

107 **C MINOR SCALE**

108 **C MINOR SCALE STUDY**

109 **ETUDE**

110 DUET

111 ETUDE

112 DUET—*While playing duets, both performers must listen critically to evaluate and adjust intonation.*

Lesson 15

113 FLEXIBILITY

114 A MAJOR SCALE AND ARPEGGIO

115 A MAJOR SCALE STUDY

Moderately ♩ = 80

116 ETUDE

Moderately ♩ = 80

117 ETUDE

Cantabile ♩. = 60

118 LONG TONES—*When playing low notes, maintain the integrity of the tone. Make sure that your low notes are not "spreading" or overblown.*

119 F# MINOR SCALE

120 F# MINOR SCALE STUDY

121 ETUDE

Lesson 16

122 **DUET**—*When playing ♪♫, remember to think of a sixteenth-note subdivision.*

123 **ETUDE**

124 **DUET**—*What musical elements in this duet make it engaging? How does the form contribute to the musical work?*

125 **ETUDE**

Lesson 17

126 FLEXIBILITY

127 A♭ MAJOR SCALE AND ARPEGGIO

A **TURN** or **GRUPPETTO** is an ornament that involves playing the written note, followed by the note above it, returning to the original note, then playing the note below it, and finally ending on the original note.

128 A♭ MAJOR SCALE STUDY

Adagio ♩ = 72

mf

129 A♭ MAJOR SCALE STUDY—*For the E♭ in measure 6, use the left E♭ key.*

Moderato ♩ = 112

mf

130 ETUDE—*This etude uses the right A♭ key. The first use is indicated with an R.*

Andante ♩ = 80

mf

continued on next page

131 F MINOR SCALE

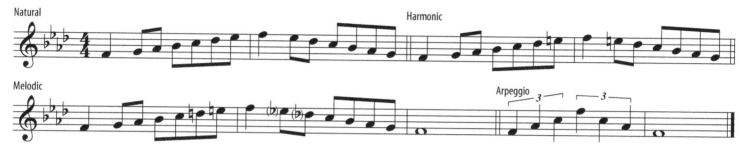

132 F MINOR SCALE STUDY

133 ETUDE—*In measure 4, roll or tip your pinky to play D♭ to C.*

Lesson 18

134 **LONG TONES**—*Play the lower octave as beautifully as possible and try to match the tone color of the higher notes to the lower octave.*

135 **FLEXIBILITY**

136 **E MAJOR SCALE AND ARPEGGIO**

137 **E MAJOR SCALE STUDY**

Moderately ♩ = 100

138 **ETUDE**

Andante ♩ = 108

mf

f

mf

139 **ETUDE**

Adagio ♩. = 60

mp *mf* *mp*

mf *mp* *mf*

mp *mf* *mp*

140 **C♯ MINOR SCALES**

141 **C♯ MINOR SCALE STUDY**

142 **ETUDE**

143 **DUET**

Lesson 19

144 **FLEXIBILITY**—*Use the first fingering on the chart in the back of this book for the high E.*

145 **ETUDE**

146 **ETUDE**

147 **ETUDE**

148 **DUET**

149 **ETUDE**

150 **DUET**—*Use critical listening to improve the performance of all musical elements in this duet.*

Lesson 20

154 ETUDE

155 DUET

156 ETUDE

157 **ETUDE**

Fanfare ♩ = 108

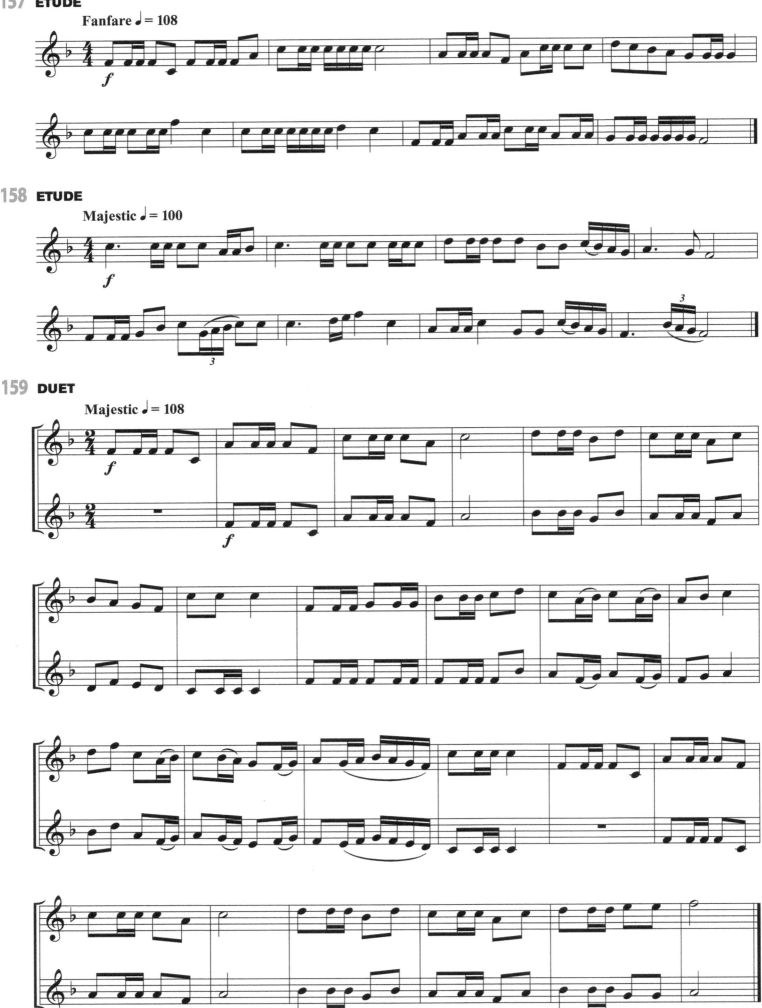

158 **ETUDE**

Majestic ♩ = 100

159 **DUET**

Majestic ♩ = 108

Lesson 21

160 **FLEXIBILITY**

161 **D♭ MAJOR SCALE AND ARPEGGIO**

162 **ETUDE**

Adagio ♩ = 66

mf

163 **ETUDE**

Andante ♩ = 100

mf

164 **B♭ MINOR SCALES**

Natural   Harmonic

Melodic   Arpeggio

165 **ETUDE**

Adagio ♩ = 66

Fine

mp

mf   *mp*

D.C. al Fine

mf

Lesson 22

166 **LONG TONES**

Slowly ♩ = 60

p — *mp* — *p* — *mf* — *p* — *f* — *p*

167 **B MAJOR SCALE AND ARPEGGIO**

168 **ETUDE**

Andante ♩ = 80

mf

cresc. *f*

169 **ETUDE**

Adagio ♩ = 72

mf

f *mf*

170 **A♭ MINOR SCALE** *(enharmonic spelling of G♯ minor)*

Natural   Harmonic

Melodic   Arpeggio

171 **ETUDE**

Adagio ♩ = 66

mf

f *mf*

f *decresc.* *mf*

Major Scales

Minor Scales

F MINOR

B♭ MINOR

E♭ MINOR

A♭ MINOR

E MINOR

B MINOR

F♯ MINOR

C♯ MINOR

G♯ MINOR

D♯ MINOR

A♯ MINOR

Oboe Fingering Chart

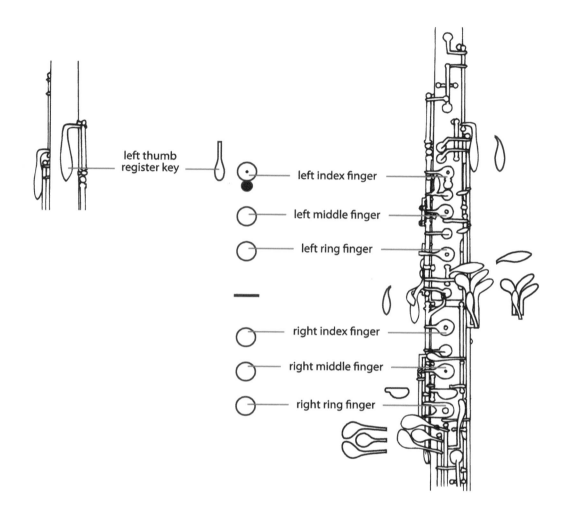

left thumb register key

left index finger

left middle finger

left ring finger

right index finger

right middle finger

right ring finger

 = open
● = pressed down

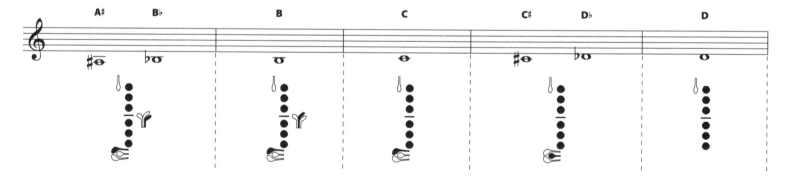

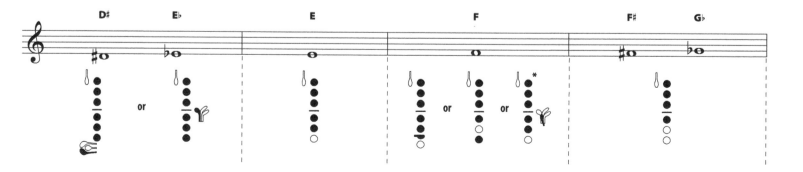

*For instruments that have this key.

48

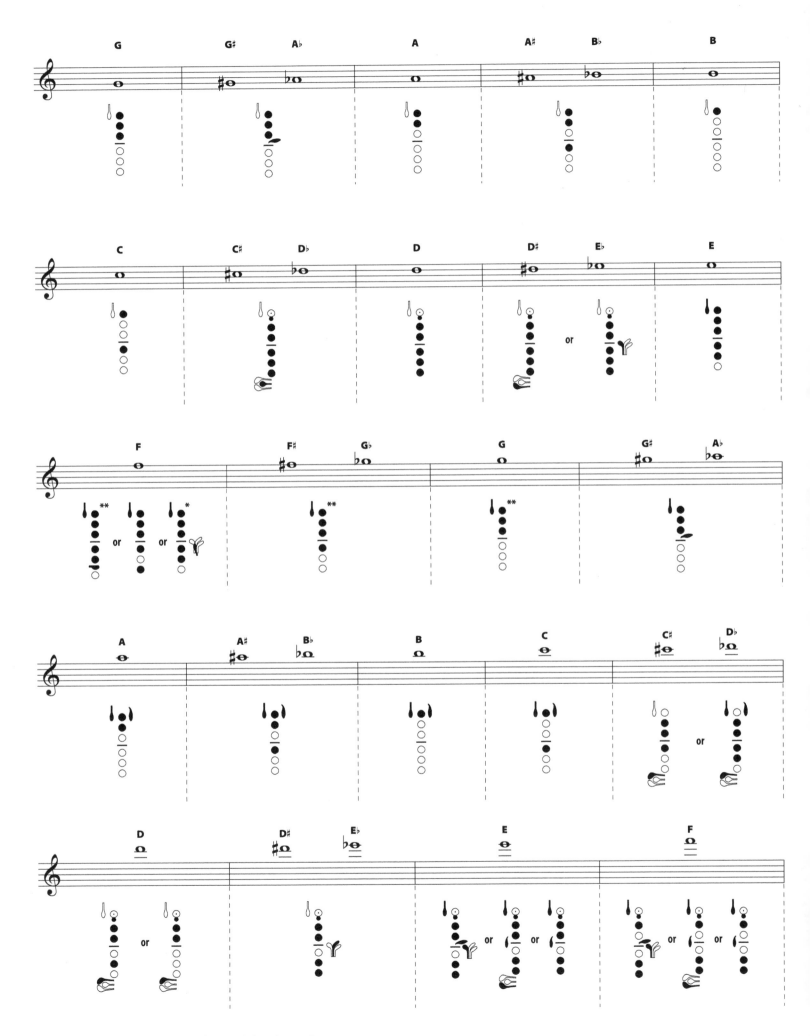

**The low B key can be added to help stabilize the pitch.